Therapy Sessions: I'm Not Who's Crazy, Everyone Else Is

Jeremy Tucker

BookLeaf Publishing

India | USA | UK

Presentation by *BookLeaf Publishing*

Web: www.bookleafpub.com

E-mail: info@bookleafpub.com

ISBN: 9789395255004

First edition 2022

DEDICATION

Everything I do is for Lariah and Suzi

ACKNOWLEDGEMENT

One of the images is one of my daughter's paintings. The painting is of an original character she created.

Introducing

Shinobi Jackson AKA the Afro-Kenshi

Created by Lariah Tucker

PREFACE

I just want to give a big shout-out to my Mama, and Blue Ridge Liquors.

Acute Paranoia Obtuse Anxiety

They will probably tell you I take it too far and I'm trippin

but not how they trying me

because a half truth's a whole lie to me

can't remember last time I got a whole night of sleep

acute paranoia obtuse anxiety

ditched the doc's prescription turned me into nobody

phew

Feels like she's flooding anytime she's riding me

she makes me cum but she never inspires me

Take It To My Grave if you ever confide in me

hard to regain trust if you ever lie to me

Delay The Landings if I'm in the pilot seat

I can show you better than I can tell you it's
nothing

can show you better than can tell you I love you

loved ones that passed on I'm still thinking of
you

Saving my checks ain't saving no woman

she says it's all mine but we still ain't going
public

if she acts brand new then I'm playing the
dumbest

Bloodlines

Got the blood of a Saint got the blood of a sinner

Got the blood of a nigga that never brought
home dinner

Got the blood of a woman that survival was
within her

Blood of a loser blood of a winner

Blood of a nigga got the blood of hunky

Blood of a square blood of a junkie

Hear my life through the paper because I bleed
what I write

Learn so much too fast like bleeding years of a
life

I got the blood of a man that I barely even know

and got the blood of a woman that refused to let
me go

Got The love from a nigga that took me in

And his family the same was treated as one of
them

so that's who I am and always have I felt

say blood thicker than water but so is milk

And the mold is sealed like bread it be on

The blood running through my veins is colder
than freon

Probably glowing like neon I stay numb to the
haters

Veins pumping through full of straight memory
erasers

Not for normal shit had too much love for some
fakers

Got the blood of what's dropping off the edge of
their bladers

And that was just food for thought being catered

I digest on it later hunting for a full stomach

Gotta have a hell of a heart for the blood that I'm pumping

An adrenaline junkie veins full of just rushing

Got the blood of a Saint got the blood of a sinner

Got the blood of a nigga that never brought home dinner

Got the blood of a woman that survival was within her

Blood of a loser blood of a winner

Blood of a nigga got the blood of honky

Blood of a squire blood of a junkie

Hear my life through the paper because I bleed what I write

Learn so much too fast like bleeding years of a life

Stuck In My Ways

Since I ain't changed the way she wanted she says nothing changed

But then complain it ain't the way it was how things just ain't the same

Say I'm so stuck in my ways

but to be the way it was is to be stuck in beginner stage

rather be stuck in my ways

Can't make up her mind there's no eyeliner for decisions

mind games that she plays promise should be in the Olympics

Smile so innocent but her heart's like the polar

I feel bliss when she f**** me good misery when she f**** me over

My heart and mind argue if it's worth it

Girl your mood swings are worse than channel
surfing

I ain't perfect but I don't pretend it

but you be acting like another person

Repeated mistakes is a decision

I hate the way you expect my forgiveness

Then play dumb to your intentions nothing to be
nothing since you want it that way

be cool when you gone as I was before you
came

At the end of the day it's just me and my ways

you stuck in a daze

we can't level up if you are still in love with the
beginner stage

Don't want it the way it was if going the way we
came

Ain't going the way we came guess I'm too stuck
in my ways

Since I ain't changed the way she wanted she
says nothing changed

Then complain it ain't the way it was how things
just ain't the same

Say I'm so stuck in my ways

but to be the way it was is to be stuck in
beginner stage

rather be stuck in my ways

Stains On My Brain

Every morning I wake up to start a new day

Puffing a huge J

until I'm droop faced

Most wouldn't make it a mile in these flu games

Some that never grew they gone say you
changed

Now I got some old friends showing new hate

Don't know why they're tripping untied shoelace

Only time I'm tripping it's to a new state

Always handle business before a cute face

Because a cute face turns two-faced

Innocent smile turned out ruthless

I run the play they played they didn't know

I get my cut then it's which way did he go

It's Cali vibes whenever I hit the smoke

exotic indica with flakes of indigo

For the bullshit my tolerance is minimal

for the Mula my mindset residual

ain't really got patience for those who listen slow

signal the call and then I run the give and go

easy as finger rolls when shooting a 3

once I realized got nobody but me

she got me always provide for my seed

probably ain't a daddy prouder than me

her mama can't stand how she came out like me

I really can't stand her mama at all

but if she needs something she can just call

put me on child support she takes a loss

remember when those threats used to throw me off

If she put me on child support she take a loss

Some of the other stains on my brain

People try to play dumb they're not as good as me

most of my exes want nothing to do with me

mad I beat them to the punch on some shit they would do to me

decided on losing them instead of losing me

but that's all old news I'm on to newer things

I'm a whole newer me I had to change my whole mindset

because no one knows how much time's left

can't waste a second trying to live better

I swear they couldn't see me with the third letter

and they've been talking shit since forever

I'm built to win I whether any weather

Eating good baby extra lemon pepper

about these women don't sweater I let her

go back the way you came if you can't take
Direction

for me pleasure is pain for her the pain is the
pleasure

because she only shows respect when she's
disrespected

it doesn't look like it the times that I'm stressing

on mood stabilizers and anti-depressants

J full of pressure joint full of nitro

some think I'm gifted some think I'm psycho

stains on my brain I can't say which one's right
though

I just wish I knew a way they could wipe off

I just wish I knew a way they could wipe off

I just wish I knew a way they could wipe off

Writings On The Wall

Now we got a storied past read the writings on
the wall

It says whose fault is more important than it
getting resolved

Take pride in the last word holds most
importance of all

never admit you're wrong and know that this
won't work

So Says the writings on the wall

Just read the writings on the wall

It's in the writings on the wall

Just read the writings on the wall

Defensive discussions when the views are just so
different

two parts to conversation but can't either of us
listen

Just to come to an agreement seems like the
main thing we are missing

only opposing opinions seem like every time we
talk

So Says the writings on the wall

Just read the writings on the wall

It's in the writings on the wall

Just read the writings on the wall

All the times I apologized for what's in the past
so distant

You act like that's your free pass to out of
nowhere start tripping

Ask how can we make it last you act like it's
none of your business

well s***, f*** trying to fix that

I say I love you and you smacking your lips
back

that's been done you ain't over that bitch yet
why you ain't over that b**** yet

I don't bring up who you let get their dick wet
I don't be bringing that s*** up

always saying I ain't right you could have been
left

this ain't how it started off

wait how'd the love get so lost

Says the writing's on the wall

Just read the writings on the wall

Read how we jumped in head first we weren't
ready at all

could tell us nothing at all

Euphoria, one accord, together in this free fall

let's rewrite this on the wall

because we write what's on the wall

the same story's been way too long

this book is about to close

without new writings on the wall

let's write new writings on the wall

because we write what's on the wall

Same story's been way too long
this book is about to close

without new writings on the wall

let's write new writings on the wall

because we write what's on the wall

For Those Who Love Me, I Love You

For those who love me I love you

for those who judge me f*** you

for those who love me I love you

for those who judge me fuck you

Might be false but you are who you hang with
that's how people view it

can't forgive whoever says they'll do better when
they already knew it

what it look like I'm stupid

how are you sorry turn around go right back and
do it

keep it moving before I lose it

I'm a f*** around and lose it going through it
trying to get it

through the lows I be high as Jimi Hendrix

through the highs eyes low as hitting switches

cut from a different linen

going hard until I finish and I'm in it when they
drop my casket

Hometown local artist Everybody is the hardest
but inside at the heart of plastic

The game Og's didn't pass it but still they looked
up to

It made a ruthless youth because they ain't teach
me they dooped for loot

And all the love was lost like a tooth was loose

so how I lace my boots

I was thrown to the Wolves wanna trade my
shoes

And be born to lose

but it's cool because I'm built to win
death took some friends

I war with a sin

I doubted God when I hit rock bottom
but he showed me that he got me
and he made me Rock Solid
can't nothing pierce the skin

when you are born to lose built to win

if you let the world tell it I was built in sin

my daughter came the same way I guess I built a
trend

so why the hell I don't feel guilty then

because I ain't out here watching
what's in everybody's closet
when I have my own skeletons

For those who love me I love you

for those who judge me f*** you

for those who love me I love you

for those who judge me fuck you

Promise love those who love me

f*** those who judging

My shoes you ain't trucked in

I done lived with nothing to lose reflex to say
f*** it

doing like a hundred down the path to
self-destruction

Watch who's coming to your Aid

because some don't come to help they come to
do the same

With a smile to hide the pain

that hurts so bad there ain't nothing you can take

but there's something you can drink and there's
something you could drain

none make it stay away

Glad I'm past those days

confused didn't know what

had some people like hold up

All my prayer soldiers

For them the love that I got it would take two
lifetimes to show it

I just try to pay it forward

For my people still down there don't want to
come out of that hole yet

But I can't want for them

I can only pay it forward

like my prayer soldiers and the people like hold
up

for them the love that I got it would take two life
times to show it

For the people like hold up

It's a chip on my shoulder and my prayers
soldiers

I just try to pay it forward for my people still
down there don't want to come up out of that
hole yet

For those who love me I love you

for those who judge me f*** you

for those who love me I love you

for those who judge me fuck you

Overreaction

Any time she tell me that it's over

Really an overreaction

Dick or some dope she gon call the next time
she wanna relapse

She like the scripts I'm eating the caps

Like a dog drinking water when I eat the cat

Hit her eject button I hit from the back

She kick down say don't worry bout kicking
back

Or Any time she tell me that it's over

Really an overreaction

Dick or some dope she gon call the next time
she wanna relapse

She like the scripts I'm eating the caps

Like a dog drinking water when I eat the cat

Hit her eject button I hit from the back

She kick down say don't worry bout kicking
back

Can't tell if she loves me or she loves to hate me

From elated to all out of patience

It's like my peace being held for ransom
The say life's a bitch but she come out them
panties

It is what it is we ain't taking no plan b

She says she loves me does she understand me

How can she make me happy won't make a
sandwich

Got the type of heart built for a mammoth

Type of liver see tequila and slam it

On the type of flights they delay the landings

I'm built to win be the last man standing

Got enough tree ain't gotta leave to go camping

Spark it up keep it on burning

I love when she keep giving head

Even she see that I'm already squirming

One thing about life you get what you deserving
What you deserving

And nothing's given you got to go earn it

I pay no mind to the s*** don't concern me

It ain't bout what you know it's bout what you
purchase
It's bout what you purchase

Yeah that pussie good but ain't buying no Birkin

Stay getting a bag but it's never new purses

Any time she tell me that it's over

Really an overreaction

Dick or some dope she gon call the next time she wanna relapse

She like the scripts I'm eating the caps

Like a dog drinking water when I eat the cat

Hit her eject button I hit from the back

She kick down say don't worry bout kicking back

Or Any time she tell me that it's over

Really an overreaction

Dick or some dope she gon call the next time she wanna relapse

She like the scripts I'm eating the caps

Like a dog drinking water when I eat the cat

Hit her eject button I hit from the back

She kick down say don't worry bout kicking back

Future's Past

Why when I'm without it I miss it

But when I got it it's nothing

Why does it become more tempting

When told to stay away from it

Why did we grow so distant
Seems that all changed in an instant
Feeling stayed you left I'm tripping
Had my back and held me down

But gave into opinions
Allied with who's against us
Now it's you who's against us
Holding me back and keep me down

Must've had doubts from beginning
Because you start way you finish
I wouldn't rebuild them bridges
If you willing come back around

Was everything that I wanted
So hard to show you was nothing

had to be done but was fronting
  remember was hard to smile

My future your past my future your past

The feeling still present how long will it last

Until my past is your future now my past is your
future

Got some one new I'm use to you're just
someone I used to

My future your past my future your past

The feeling was present but it didn't last

Now my past is your future now my past is your
future

Got someone new I'm used to you're just
someone I used to

My future your past the feeling was present

But it didn't last like bliss in the beginning

It went nowhere fast it went nowhere fast

Turned all them cares to ash I burned them all to
ash

Created more friction in the end we crashed it

But ain't no hard feelings good while it lasted

Nights full of passion your River to Rapids

Only thing that kept us in it if ain't f****** we
clashing

Now you know where my past is your future
your future

Got someone new I'm used to you're just
someone I used to

Felt a way about it first because I didn't want to
lose you

Decision made easy brought more stress than
improvements

All you had to do was play your position

But play games like we was everybody's
business

Let them in when we make peace your fam ain't
as forgiving

Since they can do what I can for you f*** your
siblings

My future your past my future your past

The feeling still present how long will it last

Until my past is your future now my past is your
future

Got some one new I'm use to you're just
someone I used to

My future your past my future your past

The feeling was present but it didn't last

Now my past is your future now my past is your
future

Got someone new I'm used to you're just
someone I used to

Just a Nigga

When I look at my daughter feel my spirits lifted

When I look at the mirror I see a statistic

When I look at the judge was never as a witness

If I know I don't have what he wants I won't be in attendance

Rather him to hold a grudge than hold me in detention

What's Rolled in my joint is opposite the 5th amendment

Three fifths descendant

 mixed with blood of those who were lynching

Used to think first of the niggas started cotton pickers

From a history class that kept half of history hidden

Only half my history I'm half white but still just
a nigga

Pessimistic living conditions breeds a product

Still choose the path you take but most gon
choose how they brought up

When you're any other race you stay molded

But When you just a nigga, another nigga is
your opponent

And I'm just another nigga

I am I I'm just a nigga

Even the richest nigga he just a nigga

Even who don't admit it he just a nigga

It's some who forget it until he just a nigga

When you just a nigga another nigga is your
opponent

And I'm just another nigga

Afraid to Love

I'm just afraid to love

Because before love been so foul

Say she appreciate the things I do, but still feel like I hold out

Ask why I can't just love, Baby I don't know how

Ask why I can't let her love me, because her expectations sprout

And I'm afraid to love

Plus this Era Mary go round

And how could I confess forgotten thrills I never told bout

If I had now what I had then and knew then what I know now

Would probably be less trusting

I ain't afraid to lose you, I'm just afraid to love

This Era so artificial ain't nothing simple

Era of hardened hearts, don't say I miss you

Cus any emotion shown is just held against you

But we won't show until later was ammunition

Can never find common ground

but always can lose our temper

Tonight was so close last night acted so distant

Might still need you like I breathe you won't
make an issue

Cus any emotion shown is just held against you

Sometimes I want a wife but settle many nights
for a nympho

Cus I never been the type to judge what you
been through

Long as you keep everybody out of what we into

And don't expect me pretend to make it
something it wasn't

Flip the script and baby ima play the dumbest

Trend to be unfaithful that's why I'm afraid to
love ya

We can keep it secret baby we just won't discuss
it

Deceit can really cut ya

I ain't afraid to lose you I'm just afraid to love ya

I'm just afraid to love

Because before love been so foul

Say she appreciate the things I do, but still feel
like I hold out

Ask why I can't just love, Baby I don't know
how

Ask why I can't let her love me, because her
expectations sprout

And I'm afraid to love

Plus this Era Mary go round

And how could I confess forgotten thrills I never
told bout

If I had now what I had then and knew then what
I know now

Would probably be less trusting

I ain't afraid to lose you, I'm just afraid to love

Put It On Me

If she really put it on me she want me to stay

If I put it on her though when I leave it's okay

Then I start to leave garments falling apart for
me

Make it hard to leave start thinking if it can wait

About to roll after pre-rolls

She like wait before you go let me stroke your
ego

And how could I turn down a smile so deceitful

About to dive off the deep end

Though I show her I want her make sure she
know I don't need it

2nd thoughts pop up when she pops out Victoria
secret

Then she show me I need it

She gives me strength and then makes me
surrender to weakness

Supposed to been gone an hour

Rolled tree the only way leaving

That little p**** got some power

Forecast for heavy rains but started a light
shower

Got her legs vibrating like when the ringer is on
silent

Rule her seas like a pirate then we fire up sour

Damn was supposed to be leaving

That little p**** got some power

If she really put it on me she want me to stay

If I put it on her though when I leave it's okay

Then I start to leave garments falling apart for
me

Make it hard to leave start thinking if it can wait

No Silver Silverware

I work so hard to reset my mindset to abundant
life

They miss the old me from up the street

But he's not far just moved right up in price

Can't run from Nana if you run from a fight

I come from nothing we had next to nothing
But we still finna share

Most can't even bare what made me a bear

Where I come from ain't no silver silverware

Never had shit I come from nothing

Coming up I looked up to some junkies

That still could handle daily functions

Taught me the art of con artist
Taught me to hold water

How to break a promise
That's why my mama is where I learned honor

My big cousin taught me respect ain't thru
gossip

And my word is bondage yeah my word is
bondage

Don't let me start on my Nana

Told me my dick gon fall off with no condom

Told me don't have no kids she not gon watch
em'

Hurt it's ironic now she always watching

She was so hard to learn to live without

To spend one day would spend any amount

Just to sit back and hear her cus me out

Soaked up so much game from those
conversations

Told me she loved me and try to have patience

Even though she knows that's not in my nature

Ways I was raised are ways I hold sacred

Ways they raised now are ways that's fugazi

I work so hard to reset my mindset to abundant
life

They miss the old me from up the street

But he's not far just moved right up in price

Can't run from Nana if you run from a fight

I come from nothing we had next to nothing
But we still finna share

Most can't even bare what made me a bear

Where I come from ain't no silver silverware

Surrender To The Mirror

Remember the day I surrendered to the Mirror

 I said I can't keep being at war with you

Now me and you on one accord ain't no more quarrels

Against the world and all we got is me and you

That's all we need we gon be cool

first thing we need a long arm spoon

and keep our foot pressed down on necks like wearing shoes

Remember that day I surrendered to the Mirror

 I said I can't keep being at war with you

I'm at an age now when younger didn't think I would make it

Path to self-destruction we holding races

tormented Souls with smiles on our faces

No Place To Belong

No place to call home

except the path where we hold the races

All here feel a pain the kind of hurt they don't
make a medication

Cigarettes soaking for mind alteration

All us ain't make it some reached the destination

Don't ask for we take it, was risking our years

And if tomorrow I wake up was my biggest fear

I grew a cold nature had to feast with the beasts

No remorse for my peers

Was at war with the Mirror

So if it's down to you and me ain't nothing to say

Ain't nothing to hear

Doing 100 down the path to self-destruction

With no one to steer

After so many races you realize that nobody here

Is coming aide

Nobody come down this path to help

They all coming to do the same

I wanted another way so decided to turn back

Said we all gotta turn around

Was treated like a turncoat

Facing all turned backs

Remember the day I surrendered to the Mirror

 I said I can't keep being at war with you

Now me and you on one accord aint no more quarrels

Against the world and all we got is me and you

That's all we need we gon be cool

first thing we need a long arm spoon

and keep our foot pressed down on necks like
wearing shoes

Remember that day I surrendered to the Mirror

 I said I can't keep being at war with you

Black Lives Matter, Really A Rumor?

This A cold world that we live in

My country got a corrupt ass system

Why they close so many schools and open
prisons

The extermination of n****** is publicized on
live television

from Usual Suspects to regular victims

and it's usually nothing happening to their killers

they get a paid vacation labeled a suspension

Had to cage my rage and now they finally
suppressed it

see it daily same s*** and instead of arrested

New graves that they dig and it bring up the
question

Like where's the Improvement?

black lives matter and that's really a rumor

And it's not just cops black lives be the shooter

And what's worse is our ways go to Junior

 so jr, he grow up to shoot another Junior

compare how we treat the hood to protesting
Troopers

 make the youth no their worth and the weight it
carries

if we don't give a f*** then why would a sheriff

Why would a judge prosecutor or a jury

 and won't be no hurry till your release date

there are still slave plantations standing in each
state

 state property aint supplies for a clean place

Untitled

I could talk about how Malcolm was a martyr

Or speak about how Martin was a dreamer

I could tell the kids don't do drugs

But they say that you should practice what you preachin

Could tell you that this is the land of the free

and the land with the most in prison

Could tell you about how history repeats

And how the clan used to hold public lynchings

But now they don't wear no white sheets

They walk around with a badge and a pistol

I turned to my n**** what you think

He looked back and said n**** where the b******

I start thinking that I'm thinking too hard

This shit will never make a difference

Voices telling me to change the world drowned
out by voices saying n**** where the b******

Should I only care where I'm about to kick it

 or what I'm spending on the weekend

I'll give you reasons that I let go of religion

And how I'm so much more in tune with spirit

I wish I could explain

No I don't m*********** I know you don't
want to hear it

That ain't right jerm you should be in church

I looked back and said n***** where the
b******

If you don't like it well you know where you can
stick it

Any questions

I could tell you about complete euphoria and
Bliss

or talk about depression

Can tell you that it burns pissing when you stick
your dick in different women no protection

We lost Uncle Leon

to AIDS in 09

sometimes like I ain't see a message

Guess I ain't no better what the b******

Forever

I'm young for my mental they want to be young
forever

All you got to do is die and you stay that young
forever

There's some people my age twice they going to
be young forever

Basically another word for dumb you stay young
forever

If you're black serving the white get life don't
come home forever

If you are white touching on tykes some make it
home for dinner

Higher ups like Donald Trump they live with
dream forever

Unarmed Target trayvon Martin stay 17 forever

S**** on my mind like every night to go to
sleep takes forever

To clear my mind reach for a light brain cells
been through genocide

Low key should have OD'd a hundred times but
now I'm better

Done enough drugs for two lives probably be
numb forever

But I kicked what I was weak to I won't be dumb
forever

 told me Jesus was our savior we've been waiting
forever

 told me one day we'll have equal rights but it's
taking forever

Forever ever

Forever ever

Forever eve

Microwave Era

Home cooked out the oven it puts a taste in the air

Microwave ain't as good but half the time to prepare

Hell of a generation gap between my parents and peers

S*** we always in a rush we're from the microwave era

When we weak for our lust but we wise for our years

And we all got damaged trust because loyalty rare

They told us life ain't Fair that's what they used to say

But everybody gets the same amount of seconds a day

It's a cold cold world but I'm going to be okay

All this wait in on my shoulders I hope it ain't
too late

Someone's always had it harder so I never
complain

Normal person couldn't deal with all the stains
on my brain

Normal person would have been killed from
s*** that been in my veins

It was to help me forget what's driving me
insane

My era kills for a name like it's something to
prove

So what's important to you to them it's nothing
to lose

This the microwave era

Everything That I Write

Everything that I write from the things in life
that I chose

Why my mind ain't all the way right

how my heart turned all the way cold

It's so hard to not trust a soul

It's so hard to not trust a soul

I'm used to hidden agenda

From people I used to be friends with

Used to not going to church because they used to
call me a sinner

Ain't no use to about that but look like a saint
when I'm grinning

And ain't never tried to go back because you
start the way that you finish

Came across some different women some with
evil ways and some heaven sent

Some I dicked down so good didn't ever have to
pay no rent

Got ditched by who I want and who wants me
got ditched it didn't make no sense

Caught up wanting what I can't have when I
could have had it like take your pic

Pass up on that and it can make you sick

To help get over the pain I was on that Jose
cuervo sip

Just waiting to catch that drain

Blow more tree than the forests in Maine

Got to struggle before success is attained

My brain is covered in some hurtful truth and
you can't remove these stains

Hear all these lies then realize everybody's doing
the same

Everything that I write from the things in life
that I chose

 Why my mind ain't all the way right

how my heart turned all the way cold

It's so hard to not trust a soul

It's so hard to not trust a soul

In life we're owed nothing but an ending

Had a knack for bad decisions

Weight of the world I couldn't lift it

Daughter got here the first few years in a losing
battle with addiction

Destroyed her chances being raised in a house
where both her parents live in

Now the way it's got to be stepparents in family
pictures

Repeated life cycle so vicious

My grandpa ain't f*** with no niggas

Until one created in his image

I never felt no hate just love he would give us

By some vibes on that side some show love and
some put up with us

Since I felt some felt that way

I just stopped going for Christmas

Stopped showing up for Thanksgiving

After years I changed my decision

From distant and apart so my seed could love
who's no different

The rest would never speak their heart

Different blood within who I consider kin they
raised and made me a part

Of them since before I was old enough to hold
farts

It's f***** up I don't feel any love towards
siblings from my father except for the only one
that I've met

It's so many of us I've only met one

And I feel love for her but as far as the rest go

 how can you feel love for anyone or anything
you don't know

Everything that I write from the things in life
that I chose

 Why my mind ain't all the way right

how my heart turned all the way cold

It's so hard to not trust a soul

It's so hard to not trust a soul

Never About Us

This was never really about us

It was either about me or you

When everything was all about me

You acted like everything was cool

About you is how I made it about us

Then you start acting like you were through

And now you want to make it about trust

But when we met you was somebody else's boo

This was never really about us

It was either about me or you

Women deceitful I can't talk I ain't right neither

Believed pretty Little liars been wrapped around some fingers

And don't just want I need her

Every time we together feel my flesh getting weaker

Even when I'm mad at her her kiss makes me surrender

Relationship was built on sex and she was no beginner

Was Caught up in my feelings with her

She let someone else in her

I felt a rage I never felt

a voice said temper temper

Never felt a pain like so

The pain of someone never admitting some s*** you know

I had to face the facts and let the worst sink in my soul

AT FIRST IT HURTS SO SO BAD
then it ain't hurt no mo

Guess I just had to wake up

There's no lipstick for decisions her mind she
can't make up

Now one way that I show it's nothing when I say
don't wait up

If she say that she love me leave her picking her
face up

Like what's this really about

Start talking about trust

Then I start thinking about us

Like

This was never really about us

It was either about me or you

When everything was all about me

You acted like everything was cool

About you is how I made it about us

Then you start acting like you were through

And now you want to make it about trust

But when we met you was somebody else's boo

This was never really about us

It was either about me or you

Untitled

From where you lose all your air that's the price of showing love

Ruthless youth from all the s*** they're tired of

Strung out on heavy drugs can't ever get enough

They're just following the footsteps of to who they looked up

They were supposed to teach me

But I'll learn the hard way them m*********** deceived me

How could I have a hard day when it ain't ever been easy

What's out the norm about that

Yeah I roll the best joints but ain't no awards for that

You can't put that on the app

That thought shows I don't know s***

And I'm just one of many men I guess that's just
the motion

Tell my brother about better Days but really I
feel it's hopeless

Can't let his heart get cold as mine and don't
know no emotion

Not a product of my environment this life was
chosen

Better judgment didn't come around til I was a
little older

And you won't ever hear me complain because
you ain't supposed to

I play my part everyone else wants to be lacosta
nostra

So common snorting coke up

I knew a high School freshman do it till he
throw up

Take a second to catch his breath and refill his
nose up

Try to tell him thee's more to life

He said who the f*** are you and the
importance of your advice

He said you're not s*** already and you ain't
even 25

He said to him the difference between wrong
and right

Told me it ain't one said there's only decisions

Told him the difference is some decisions are
harder to live with

He went back in his pack oh so you going to
make a difference

I hear you talking like that but you see how we
living

I said the way you thinking man is going to be
worse for our children

He told me so he'll probably be gone before a
chance to conceive one

It's f***** up cuz I believe him
Don't know if he learned to listen

But he won't hear me out since I've been caught
up in the system

Said only reason we speaking cuz you f******
my sister

Told him I'm not against you but he probably
right

He only seen me come over the wee hours of the
night

The type of s*** we used to discuss on the paper
flight

What some see as f***** up to me a day in the
life

Life only hard as you make it just better rolls of
the dice

Life's only hard as you make it just better rolls
of the dice

Forever In A Day/Flower Petal Thoughts

Forever In A Day

If we could fit forever in a day

When the nightfall came still want you to stay

Hate when you leave love watching you walk away

In those jeans it's barely space if you can fit in them

Then we could fit forever in a day

When the nightfall came still want you to stay

Hate when you leave love watching you walk away

In those jeans it's barely space if you can fit in them

Then we could fit forever in a day

Flower Petal Thoughts

How did I get caught

Up in these flower petal thoughts

She loves me she loves me not
Really only she knows

But when she let down her guard underneath
she's Stone of heart

It's like plucking flower petals from a concrete
Rose

The heart refuse to see what the mind already
knows

That the pain of holding on can be way worse
than letting go

How did I get caught

Up in these flower petal thoughts

She loves me

 she loves me not

She loved me

She loved me not

She loves me

She loves me not